Going With the Post Workflow:

How to Rock as a

Television & Film

Assistant Editor

By Ashley E. Alizor, M.F.A

Ashley E. Alizor

Copyright © 2018 Ashley E. Alizor

ISBN-13:
978-1718973688

ISBN-10:
1718973683

Going With the Post Workflow:
How to Rock as a Television & Film Assistant Editor

Introduction

"Going With the Post Workflow: How to Rock as a Television & Film Assistant Editor," is a carry along technical manual for all Television and Film Editors.

To gain that prestigious title of Editor many of us begin as Night Assistant Editors and some of us as Production Assistants. Then, we make the climb to Junior or Apprentice Editor and then to Editor after many years of practice, networking and hard work. Not to mention the pitfalls and failures that even the most skillful and creative Editors meets along their long pathway toward their dream.

In "Going With the Post Workflow: How to Rock as a Television & Film Assistant Editor," I explain concepts that many of my interns in their Senior year as Undergraduates at Universities do not know. Everything in this first chapter should be understood by you before taking a job at any post facility even as a Production Assistant.

Chapter 1 covers the basics of importing and exporting media into the various system and software in an organized manner, this is also known as Media Management. Chapter 2 is about Codecs and what file extensions tell us about the media that we have been given from the set or that we are simply downloading. Chapter 3 dives into Software and programs that you should own and practice every day with at home. The more software you learn to be comfortable with, the more valuable you are to your employer.

Chapter 4 is all about my own anecdotal experiences, shadowing and being shadowed in Post Production. Shadowing is a term that means to observe or follow someone around at work in order to get a glimpse of their daily tasks and activities and better understand the Craft of Editing.

Chapter 5 recaps and reviews what we learned in this book and gives examples of when you will utilize this knowledge working in Television and Film at Post Production facilities.

There is a Glossary at the end of this book to help you familiarize yourself with the many of these terms and concepts that you will encounter in the Industry.

Assistant Editing is always changing essentially at the rate of technology itself but this book will help you concepts tried and true from a working TV and Film Editor.

So, here you have it: my own real world bits of technical knowledge for all to grow and know. Remember that this book is an overview, so if you would like to learn more about The Craft of Editing check back for more technical manuals in the future.

Acknowledgements

Thank you to my truly extraordinary parents Evelyn Matchen and John O. Alizor, PhD, you are my rock. I am grateful to my wonderful and supportive siblings; my sisters Alexis and Alyssa Alizor are amazing filmmakers as well and my brother John O. Alizor, Jr. is a wonderful and talented person. Thank you to my rescue dog King Kingston.

Thank you to my readers who embark on this journey into the Television and Film Industry. This is the Technical Computer NLE Editing Instructional Manual book that you have been looking for in a quick 35 page read you can carry along that you can take with you on your phone. In this book you get diagrams, images and a concise glossary of editing terms in one place, at your fingertips. I greatly appreciate every one of my readers.

A special thank you to the Editing Faculty at the University of Southern California, where I received my Masters of Fine Arts in Film and Television Production. At USC I got to be a Teaching Assistant to some of the brightest young minds under some of the most well achieved and talented Filmmakers; Bruce Block, John Rosenberg, Stephen Lovejoy, A.C.E., Norman Hollyn, and Reine-Claire.

I also wish to thank my peers and colleagues who share my passion for editing and explored it with me in my career specifically Dominique Ulloa, Ciaran Vejby and Michele Lane.

Thank you!

Ashley E. Alizor, M.F.A.
University of Southern California
USC Master of Fine Arts '15
Television and Film Production

CONTENTS

Ashley E. Alizor

1

MEDIA MANAGEMENT

The reason that **Media Management** is the first topic that we cover is because as many Assistant Editors will tell you it's the most important thing to plan for. How much media do you have to import? How much space is available for that import onto the **Hard Drive**? Which of the Many hard drives on the Server should this media be placed on before I import it?

If we don't ask these questions before we start than our Editing Project risks having a whole lot of missing and misplaced media scattered across hard drives. when we return we see the dreaded "Media Offline."

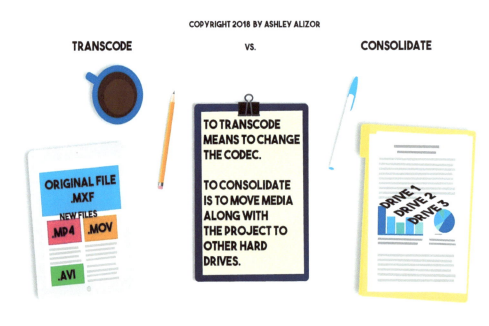

TRANSCODE VS. **CONSOLIDATE**

ORIGINAL FILE
.MXF
NEW FILES
.MP4 .MOV
.AVI

TO TRANSCODE MEANS TO CHANGE THE CODEC.

TO CONSOLIDATE IS TO MOVE MEDIA ALONG WITH THE PROJECT TO OTHER HARD DRIVES.

DRIVE 1
DRIVE 2
DRIVE 3

So, you don't have to hunt media down later it is a good idea to practice your Media Management skills and organize yourself now.To check the available space before any import or export on any hard drive on a MAC we right click on the mouse and then choose "Get Info." On a Windows

Operating System go into your Control Panel and find the hard drive and navigate to "Properties," click on that to see the available and original hard drive space. From here we can compare the hard drive with the Media Card to see if we need more space – otherwise the transfer will fail.

The other option it too **Transcode** the media, which means to change the codec, size, resolution or frame rate in order to make a very large files editable in the system and software that we are using. When you transcode media, new files are generated by the computer that are the same files but easier to edit because instead of 4k Apple Prores 4444 now they are 2k - 1920 x 1080 or instead of Compressed Quicktimes – H.264 .mov they are back to their original 4k camera format.

You can use Avid Media Composer or Adobe Media Encoder to

COPYRIGHT 2018 BY ASHLEY ALIZOR

transcode and consolidate media. To **Consolidate** Media, means that you are moving all or some of the media to a new drive so someone can edit it from that drive. You may be asked to **AMA Link** the footage, this is a type of importing that points at the footage and saves time rather than copy the footage to an actual shared drive.

Avid Media Composer and **Adobe Premiere** automatically AMA link in AVID but in different ways. They are automatically created by the software as duplicate files and then even saved onto your system or hard drive as high resolution DNxHd .mxf files that are easily editable by the software itself.

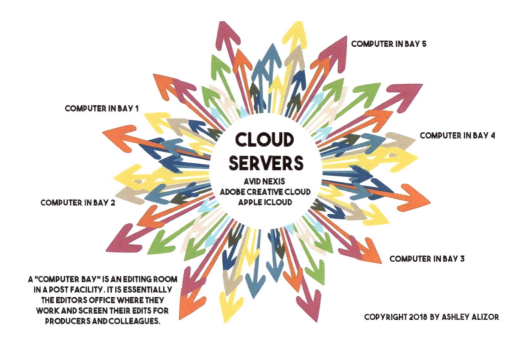

Remember to utilize automated **Grouping** software and bots to do the heavy lifting when possible and save even more time and energy.Save yourself time by **AMA linking** but only if you know the drive is always going to be mounted there and never ever moved from that system or you will have media offline.

Checking your Disk Space before you start any editing process to write or read from that hard drive is a great idea. Keep in mind that most companies have literally hundreds of hard drives and as an Assistant Editor it is your job to keep track of where every project and its corresponding raw original media lives at all times. To help you keep track of the many hard drives and Thumbnail aka Memory Stick Drives, generate an Excel Spreadsheet with the Date, The Name of the Drive, Drive Capacity, Available Size and a quick description.. Doing this seemingly never ending yet fun and meditative job is an entry level position, which people do get specifically hired to do; this is referred to as "Working in the Vault".

Every Production Company in the world has an archive or a room called the **Vault** where they archive all of their past Projects, Outputs and even some raw original media on tapes and hard drives if they have that kind of space. Eventually many of the hard drives are transferred to LTO Tape and then reused for new projects. Again that would be your job as an Assistant Editor working in the vault. Getting a job in the vault is a great way to become really good at Media Management and someday you could even end up as the "Head of Production Operations" at a studio.

When you go to a new company it is alright to ask a lot of questions about where they want every bit of media for each project. This will make sure that you or your Editor (s) do not run into any issues down the line that could cause delays to finishing the edit. Finishing requires that all things concerning the media was done in an organized manner from the very beginning, more on this later.

Cloud Servers such as the robust Avid Nexis Client Manager or Adobe's Creative Cloud are used at Production companies as an alternative to having multiple physical hard drives. A **Computer Bay** is essentially the Editor's office, it is a fully operating room where a computer and it's speakers and monitors are stored and maintained daily by the assistant editor. A Cloud Server is a Network of hard drives that can be accessed from many different Computer Bays because it is not plugged into anyone of them but rather connected to all of them through the company wifi or ethernet network. This Network of hard drives lives in a digital storage space called a cloud, so to speak, so that everyone can edit from the same place without having to move that media anywhere.I created an Acronym to help remember the size of files and the calculate the space of whether my media will fit on my hard drive or not.

Keep Making Good Time
Parties!

KB	(Kilobytes)	**K**eep
MG	(Megabytes)	**M**aking
GB	(Gigabytes)	**G**ood
TB	(Terabytes)	**T**ime
PT	(Petabytes)	**P**arties

*Each time we go up it's by 1,000 Kilobytes. Petabyte hard drives are extremely large and rarely used as it would be overkill, a 25 -200 Terabytes of space is plenty for a show or movie.

Producers will need you to email them or upload them the newest cut or file, it should never be bigger than 1 - 2 MB to be sent. You must compress your output to be able to email it. Sometimes putting it in a zipped folder will compress it enough, other times you will have to take the file into another program to compress it.

Adobe Media Encoder and Quicktime 7 are the best programs to compress video files with because they give you many options and control of the parameters. **Compression** means to make a file smaller through either zipping it or taking it into a software that will change its size to something smaller. Compressed files have lower resolution than the original one inherently but it can be emailed.

To avoid having to compress a file we will send a physical hard drive to the company requesting the file to color correct, finish or even to broadcast. We would not air a compressed video on Television or in a movie theater.

Tips and Tricks

Media Management

Tip: First thing First. Duplicate the project before you open it to make sure you can always go back to the original one. At the end of the title add your own initials, (i.e. Camry_2018_Commercial_Assist-AA).

Tip: Do not change original file names, keep everything intact and copy each name into a column or the software to be able to match back to it when it goes from offline to online and is up-resed, meaning it goes back up to 4k or higher.

Tip: Always have a personal Thumb Drive on hand just in case you need to bring media somewhere and there are no available drives in the building. People will thank you for saving the day and coming so well prepared to work.

2

CODECS

Good News! There is no need to memorize the codecs. What's really important is to know which one opens in which program, so you don't waste time guessing it. Codecs are the last part of any file name like .MXF, .MOV, .AVI, .FLV, .MPEG and .MP4 just to name a few. These file extensions or formats, tell us more about the media we are dealing with then you may think.

First off, the codec tells us the possible resolution of the file and it tells us what program most likely created that file and therefore will give you the easiest way to open or edit the file as well. Note that most video editing programs or Non- Linear Editing Systems (NLEs) can put out any video.

However, Windows Movie Maker only makes video exports that are .AVI, .MOV or .WMV and .WMV files are specifically for Windows Operating Systems and so it does not play nice in MAC Operating Systems. Be warned! The media we are given from set is Video and seperate Audio files. The audio files tend to always be .WAV or .MP3 files.

Every camera creates its own specific file and have their own specific workflow and unique pitfalls to watch out for. XDCam gives you spanned clips that are either all the same clip or the same clip cut into parts across files.What a mess! Don't panic though. To save yourself the headache you should look at the file codecs to better understand them before you begin even working with them. Once they are i8n the system check there metadate via the program properties settings and learn even more about the media before you build the project for your Editor to work with.

Codecs also have different resolutions that they are able to output. This is because codecs are essentially gift wrapping your media file in either something cheap and fast or expensive and slow. If it's being exhibited on Television or in theaters we are going to use the highest resolution possible, uncompressed of course.

Here is a list of Video and Audio codec file formats with their corresponding Software:

Software Specific Project File:

Adobe Illustrator Art (.ai)

Adobe Title Designer (.prtl)

Adobe Title Designer (.ptl)

Adobe Sound Document (.asnd)

Adobe Premiere 6 Bins (.plb)

Adobe Premiere 6 Storyboards (.psq)

Adobe Premiere 6 Projects (.ppj)

Adobe Premiere Pro Projects (.prproj)

Adobe After Effects Projects (.aep, .aepx)

Adobe Photoshop (.psd)

Avid Project (.avp)

Avid Bin (.avb)

Windows Media (.wmv,.wma,.asf,.asx)

QuickTime Movie (.3gp,.3g2)

      MPEG-4 (.m4v)

Image File:

CompuServe GIF (.gif)

TIFF image file (.tif,.tiff)

JPEG (.jpg,.jpe,.jpeg,.jfif)

Portable Network Graphics (.png)

Video File:

AVI Movie (.avi)

FLV (.flv)

P2 Movie (.mxf)

FilmStrip (.flm)

MPEG Movie (.mpeg,.mpe,.mpg,.m2v,.mpa,.mp2,.m2a,.mpv,.m2p,.m2t)

QuickTime Movie (.mov, .mp4)

FLV (.flv)

HD Movie(.mts,.m2ts)

VOB (.vob)
F4V (.f4v)
MKV (.mkv)

Audio File:
MP3 Audio (.mp3,.mpeg,.mpg,.mpa,.mpe)
Macintosh Audio AIFF (.aif,.aiff)
Windows WAVE audio file (.wav)
AAF (.aaf)

Metadata Media Document File
(Export as PDF and Excel Forms for deliverables):
Shockwave flash object (.swf)
Sony VDU File Format Importer (.dlx)
Bitmap (.bmp,. dib,.rle)
Encapsulated PostScript (.eps)
CMX3600 EDL (.edl)

Tips and Tricks

Codecs

Tip: As an Assistant Editor you don't get to make the final decision of what Codec something will be delivered in, we are instead given a long list of Deliverables, or files that the Television Network, Film Festival or Movie Studio require delivered after the project is finished in order to exhibit it on Television or theaters to the public.

3

PROGRAMS AND SOFTWARE

There are certain computer software and programs that you should own and practice with at home. I am talking about the professional programs that we use daily in the industry. The more software that you learn to be comfortable with, the more valuable you are to your employers.

Most Assistant Editor know the major NLEs – Avid, Premiere and Final Cut. You can set yourself apart and make sure that you keep working even when the initial work runs out by knowing all three of the programs listed above.One of the best, most marketable skills for one to have is to be good at Graphic Design. When we talk about Graphics in the film industry we are saying that you can build, edit, and export animated graphic elements from After Effects and then import them in for your Editor.

Many graphics have to have an **Alpha Layer**, which is an invisible layer and appears as a transparent background that can be used as an overlay and placed on top of the video. The Alpha Layer setting is in the program dialogue box when you make an Export from any NLE. Go ahead and practice your temp graphics today by placing graphics and making new ones as if you are in charge of temp visual effects. Practice! If you download Photoshop and play around in the environment it will and you create anything than you are on the right track. Assistant Editors often export already made graphics, this is called rendering out the graphics from the system into Animation quicktime video files sometimes .MOV and sometimes .TIFF files. Ask your Lead Assistant Editor or Post Supervisor what files they need **"rendered out"** from After Effects. The specifics will depend where the **Render** is being sent, posted or imported into next.

Ok, now back to the basics because still the most important Software for you to know are the main video and audio editing programs the NLEs that are named Avid, Premiere and Final Cut. Those are the big top 3. There are also important programs that work in tandem with these Non-Linear Editing Systems for an even smoother workflow. Quicktime 7 is the industry wide way to check the size of a video file. Navigate via a right-click to "Get Info" on a Mac Operating system computer. To compress it even smaller within Quicktime 7 navigate to the Export drop down menu bar and go to "Export As".There are also other free programs online that every production company uses to make their workflow work even smoother. These extra supplementary but highly useful programs really do vary from company to company so take note of any new or handy nifty ones and begin downloading them wherever you go for serious bonus points. Remember to ask permission before you download any software onto a Company computer. Also, remember to not update your software without getting explicit approval.

If you're computer program is updated but no one else's than the projects that you create will not be able to be opened by anyone not on your system. It will be like everyone's project was made with a different software. Constant software updates are rarely done at Production companies for this reason, fear of becoming incompatible with their own projects.

<u>Tips and Tricks</u>

Program & Software

Tip: Know the top NLE Video editing Software

> Avid Media Composer
> Adobe Premiere CC
> Adobe After Effects
> Adobe Photoshop
> Final Cut X

Tip: Set yourself apart by becoming great at creating and exporting graphic elements. Watch how to videos on YouTube and then just make something in After Effects. Have fun and do not let yourself feel intimidated. Go get 'em tiger!

4

HUMAN RESOURCES

Fellow Assistant Editors are your number one resource. I have called, texted and Facebook messaged other Assistant Editor colleagues who gave me answers for the low, low price of 100% free! They were also more than happy to help because they get to do some mental homework and then even hone their own skills to help you. Many respond back within minutes with follow-up questions and a few replies later, Eureka! We found the solution and we figured it out together. Of course you should ask your coworkers but remember that they have their own projects and potential issues so try not to burden them unless they offer to be your Sensei.

Asking questions at work is so important. Messing things up in such a tight deadline driven environment is not recommended. So it never hurts to send an email out that clarifies the tasks and priority.Certain tasks have priority over others. Also, emails are great tools for detailing and organizing a tasks before you begin.. Ask for clarification but only if you were taking notes. There is nothing worse than someone who doesn't take notes and then needs things explained to them further. That is never a surprise but always a symptom of someone who needs things explained to them for that reason multiple times. So please take notes and then you can at least asks questions that are actually focused.

When you are invited to watch other Editors or Assistant Editors work it is an honor and a favor to you, so remember don't talk. Watch Closely. Take Notes. Ask Questions. Go be Great! Usually I have watched other people and been fascinated by their approach to a task, which usually differs from my own approach. There are various ways to finish a tasks so stick by what has worked for you in the past. Remember that there are a trillion billion ways to skin a potato, I like this expression better than the original but you get what I am saying hopefully. Do it the way you know!

Tips and Tricks

Human Resource

Tip: Teach yourself, let others teach you and remember to teach others because that way you never stop learning new things and ways of operating these systems.

Tip: Go to Film and Television Mixers and Networking Events. Try to not be shy or get drunk. Meet as many people as possible and connect with the ones that click with you afterwards, subtly ask for their advice and see what is working for them and what is not. These events lead to friendships more often than jobs so don't go be overly professional, it will read as fake and opportunist. The funny thing is how getting to know someone in this industry feels like a breath of fresh air versus them asking you right away for a job or advice. It is also a great feeling when you make a new friend at a mixer and then later on end up working together.

5

ADVICE AND INITIAL JOB OUTLOOK

Another great feeling you will have as an Assistant Editor; finishing a project, Television Show, Movie, Web Series or a task to completion. I love my job because every day I meet several goals and feel pretty empowered and capable afterwards. Also, everyday is different and every project is unique and tells it's own story.

From the top Editor to the newest one, we are all Freelance Contractors. When the film is finished, we all go home and find another job. When the show's season ends, we all go home and wait for it to return while we work other jobs. If the show gets canceled, we all go home and collect on our own unemployment insurance till that runs out or we move onto another job.

All of this uncertainty and insecurity within the job's structure is a reality and while this may all seem scary, do not be afraid. You will get to try out different companies and build a large career network. Often, you will get hired back by the same company over and over again with a hiatus break every few weeks or months to go visit family or go on vacation. Not bad right?

Also, you will make more money as a Freelancer rather than as a Staff Assistant Editor because companies hire Freelance Assistant Editors for rushed yet huge projects and are willing to pay top dollar to bring in a couple extra good hands. I worked on the Apple iPhone Watch commercial and I made close to $7k in about three weeks working 60-70 hour weeks. I loved working Freelance. The Staff Assistant Editors made a lot less money during that time but when the iPhone commercial finally aired, I was let go of and they got to keep their job. In essence, I am a seasonal worker, which is fairly typical when working in digital, film and television post production.

<u>Tips and Tricks</u>

Initial Job Outlook

Tip: An Assistant Editor position is not for the faint of heart or the passionless. The job is very challenging, demanding and always uncertain. It is also amazingly rewarding, fun and you can make close and lasting professional relationships working long hours along some inspiring and brilliant people. The people of your post team often become like family.

Tip: Embrace the flow of things, don't fight the chaos. Try not to stress and remember to have fun and enjoy yourself everyday. We are creating and collaborating. Congratulations to you that you made it this far! Most do not.

GLOSSARY

.

Alpha Layer - a transparent background so the video can be placed as an overlay on top of video.

AMA Link - a type of importing that points at the footage and saves time rather than copying the footage to a different hard drive.

Available Disk Space - the additional space left over to fit even more media onto on that particular hard drive. Use "get info" or "properties" to view.

Cloud Servers - the Avid Nexis is an example of a cloud server, it is an alternative to having multiple physical hard drives, the cloud server is accessible via the Ethernet or WIFI.

Codecs - the file format which is indicated as the last part of the file name.

Consolidate - moving media to a new hard drive to make it accessible from a different drive.

Deliverables - files that the Television Network or Movie Studio require delivered after the project is finished in order to broadcast or exhibit it to the public.

Graphics Assistant Editor - builds, edits, or exports animated graphic elements from After Effects and then import them in for your Editor.

Hard Drive - an external or internal digital or physical place where media is stored and accessed. Must be kept cool and dry. Keep track of them using an excel spreadsheet in the vault.

Non-Linear Editing Systems (NLE) – any computer software program that you can edit together audio and video clips within.

Quicktime 7 - the industry wide way to check the size of a video file and to compress it even smaller through the "Export As" function.

Render out - export already made graphics out of the software into a folder as quicktime or tiff sequence.

Transcode - change the codec, size or frame rate of the media in order to make the very large files editable in the system and software that we are using.

Up-Res - We Upres footage from what the computer can handle to the highest form of broadcast at the end. This is done by the Online Editor. Matching back to the original footage depends on whether the Assistant Editor kept the original tape names intact within the editing system.

ABOUT THE AUTHOR

Ashley worked as a Freelance Editor in Los Angeles while earning her Masters of Fine Arts in Film in Television Production where she was also a Teaching Assistant. Years of experience as an Assistant Editor coupled with her education at USC is wrapped into the book that you hold in your hands. Ashley Alizor was born in Rancho Palos Verdes, California to the inventor of Curl Activator John O. Alizor Sr., Phd and Evelyn Louise Matchen, Fashion Designer and Hair Guru from Honolulu, Hawaii. Ashley is 1st generation Nigerian and 2nd generation African American. She has lived in Japan before.

She is the Head Art Director at Odinanii and Lets Cyber and lives with her rescue Chihuahua King Kingston Alizor who is a really wonderful and super cute companion dog who she lives with. Her fascination with film from the time of her family home movies, has blossomed into a film editing career. As a storyteller she writes about technology, artificial intelligence and futurism. Ashley Alizor is also a Film Director and Editor, Animator, Photographer, Cinematographer and Acrylic and Oil Painter, as well as a Fashion Designer. Often her muse speaks many languages.

Currently, she lives and works in Hollywood, California as an Assistant Editor in Post Production.

Thank you.

Ashley E. Alizor

www.ingramcontent.com/pod-product-compliance
Lightning Source LLC
Chambersburg PA
CBHW041153050326
40690CB00001B/463